Naughty Nonsense, Lascivious Limericks and Much More

ISBN: Hardcover   978-1-6641-0401-3
            Softcover   978-1-6641-0092-3
            eBook   978-1-6641-0091-6

Print information available on the last page.

Rev. date: 05/24/2022

To order additional copies of this book, contact:
Xlibris
AU TFN: 1 800 844 927 (Toll Free inside Australia)
AU Local: (02) 8310 8187 (+61 2 8310 8187 from outside Australia)
www.Xlibris.com.au
Orders@Xlibris.com.au
815253

Naughty Nonsense, Lascivious Limericks and Much More

David Ellis

ABOUT AUTHOR

David Ellis has from an early age been a fan of British comedians (think Frankie Howerd and the Carry On crew) and their influence can be seen in this varied selection of his comic verses of over fifty years.

He worked as an English teacher in England where he sought to encourage creative writing and an appreciation of literature, including poetry.

Well known in the UK and Australia as a Chess player, he has been West of England, Cornish, Kent and three times West Australian champion. He has competed in a number of Australian Open and Closed Championships with a best result equal 3rd. He has also regularly coached young players, including a to-be British Champion.

He has been Chess columnist for the West Australian newspaper for more than 24 years and in 2001 received the Australian Chess Federation Medal for outstanding work as a chess correspondent, the year after receiving the Queen's Australian Sports Medal.

He plays piano and has been in demand as an accompanist - in collaboration with a junior choir he recorded a 45EP and years later recorded two CDs with a soprano, Willemina Foeken.

He is father to two children. His son is a champion Ultra-Marathon runner while his daughter has competed in a number of Triathlons as well as successfully representing Western Australia in both the Girls and Womens Chess teams.

*Author with son John and daughter Tanya after
they had completed a mini triathlon in Perth.*

Illustrations are by Rosie Di Wu, an Australian illustrator currently based in Austin, Texas. She illustrated and designed the program for the 2019 Story Fest, the international performing writers' festival held annually in Sydney. Her mini-comic art about the origins of rock music in China was published in Meet Me in the Pit. She is inspired by traditional paintings, European comic art and 2D animation concept artists. In her spare time she enjoys going life drawing, attending live music gigs and travelling.

ABOUT THE BOOK

WARNING

Be prepared to be amused by the odd ways of the characters here portrayed in the first section of the book devoted to Limericks.

Be prepared to feel sympathy for their mishaps and trials.

But especially be prepared to be shocked by their goings-on and shenanigans - the forger, the glutton, the cheat, the drunkard, the proud, the greedy, the slothful, the unfaithful, the exhibitionist, the sex-mad, the dominatrix, the cougar, the transsexual, the transvestite, the masochist, the homosexual and many more.

However also enjoy the more gentle humour of the later lengthier works set both in the UK and Australia which include homages to the Australian love of sport and the beach as well as a sad childhood tale, a romance on VE Day and thoughts on Covid.

CONTENTS

NAUGHTY NONSENSE AND
LASCIVIOUS LIMERICKS

From primary school I had an interest in poetry and I could recite all eighteen verses of Lewis Carol's 'The Walrus and the Carpenter'. I also enjoyed the Nonsense Rhymes of Edward Lear which were the stimulus to write my own first Nonsense Rhyme:

> *There was an old man from Doncaster*
> *Who took a job as a school master.*
> > *He caned all the boys*
> > *Who made any noise,*
> *That nasty old man from Doncaster.*

In my last few years at secondary school my main studies were in English which included such writers as Chaucer, the Elizabethan poets, Shakespeare and Wordsworth, all of whom increased my interest in Poetry.

As a mature age student in the 1970s I studied for a Diploma in Recreation. At the end of a week's camp the group put out a magazine in which my contributions included a number of Nonsense Rhymes about some of the other students. I sought to improve on the rhyming of Lear by having a distinctly different final line which was not a virtual repeat of the first line.

Many years later at one of a number of music soirees, where I mainly acted as an accompanist to singers, I added to these to present a collection of rhymes about each of the participants. I would stress, that although I have used names of people I know, the verses are in no way meant to imply that they are guilty of any vice or weakness of character depicted in the writings.

My third burst of nonsense writing occurred prior to presentation at the West Australian Bush Poets Society. I had purchased 'The Great Australian Book of Limericks' by Jim Haynes where the content proved an encouragement to branch out into a much more risqué and bawdy content.

Since deciding to put all the verses together I have more than doubled the number.

The first true limerick, according to Jim Haynes, has been credited to Robert Herrick (1591-1674) and the limerick has been popular in all English-speaking countries ever since. Among its practitioners have been Lewis Carroll, W S Gilbert (of Gilbert and Sullivan fame), Mark Twain, T S Eliot, Ogden Nash and science fiction writer Isaac Asimov.

WARNING
Be prepared to be amused by the ways of the characters here portrayed.

Be prepared to feel sympathy for their mishaps and trials.

But especially be prepared to be shocked by their goings-on and shenanigans.

Perhaps readers may find their names in the rhymes or possibly their own personality.

SEXY SHORTS

I sometimes think sex is like food; those obsessed with it are either gluttons or are starving. Not that I am an expert on the subject. I used to think a stopcock was a chastity belt.

Are you familiar with the term spoonerism? Named after the Oxford don and ordained minister William Archibald Spooner (1844-1930), the spoonerism is an error in speech in which corresponding or near corresponding initial consanants are switched. Examples: from a teacher to his under-performing pupil - 'You have tasted the whole worm.' (wasted the whole term); A patriot shouts, 'Three cheers for our queer old dean!' (our dear old Queen). If Dr Spooner had espied a full-frontal female nude he might have explained, 'What a cunning stunt!'

A sailor was courting sweet **Sue**,
Who promised she'd always be true.
But the story is out,
Of its truth I've no doubt,
She's since slept with the rest of the crew.

That kinky young lady **Yvonne**
From a sex shop bought a strap-on.
When I asked, "Who's the buck
You're planning to fuck?"
I'm afraid she wouldn't let on.

A young masochist from **Darjeeling**
Would hang by his balls from the ceiling.
When asked if the strain
Caused him much pain,
He said, "Yes, it's a wonderful feeling."

A sex-hungry farm girl named **Kay**
Took a new lover each day.
      When they said, "You're a sinner,"
      She replied, "No, a winner
Every time I leap in the hay."

With ten inches of manhood, young **Jude**
Would strut round the streets in the nude.
      When he flaunted his tackle
      He raised everyone's hackle
And they damned him for being so lewd.

A seductive young siren named **Dixie**
Was said by the guys to be frisky.
      And to be with her alone,
      So the rumour has grown,
Would be both exciting and risky.

I confessed to my dearest friend **Jenny**
That for weeks I hadn't had any.
　　But when asked to her bed
　　I was shocked when she said,
"It'll cost you a pretty penny."

A rake who's a black market dealer
Is intent on seducing young **Sheila.**
　　He acts sad and sighs,
　　He begs and he cries,
But she still won't allow him to feel her.

Form-filling is perplexing poor **Terry**
Who's frustrated and seems so unmerry.
　　"Name, address, email, they're ok
　　But position – just what should I say?
Scrum half, mid-off, missionary?"

A gin-sodden old woman called **Suzie**
Was known as the neighbourhood floozy.
　　She said, "Any bloke
　　Can give me a poke.
At my age one cannot be choosy."

An uncouth old fellow called **Roger**
In a crowded room pulled out his todger.
　　When we shouted as one,
　　"Such a thing is not done,"
He replied, "Yes, it is and so sod'ya."

Young **Desmond** said, "I must confess
I love to be seen in a dress.
　　Add panties and bra
　　And I think I'm a star,
So please can you call me Princess?"

An excited male virgin called **Danny**
Was keen to explore the girl's fanny.
      When he reached out his hand
      To feel for her gland,
He discovered that she was a tranny.

Poor recently married young **Maude**
With sex had quickly got bored.
      She said, "I do fear
      It will soon become clear
That I am an out and out fraud."

1. A many times mother named **Jill**
Just wouldn't go on the pill.
> Since the birth of child ten
> She's at it again
And will be 'till over the hill.

And ten years later:
2."I've had eighteen children," said **Jill**,
"But I'll never go on the pill.
> And for what it is worth
> I'll keep giving birth,
For where there's a way there's a will."

I was accosted by randy old **Bert**
Who is known as a terrible flirt.
> He said, "If you're gay
> There's games we can play."
Then endeavored to lift up my shirt.

Erotic thoughts filled the mind of young **Jude**,
So he set them in verse that was rude.
> Friends who bought his anthology
> Demanded an apology,
Saying, "This is so shameless and crude."

A saucy young siren called **Rita**
After work got a colleague to meet her.
> She let her hand roam
> And said, "Come to my home.
It's more fun upon my three-seater".

At the museum enamoured young **Liz**
Gave her boyfriend a lengthy french kiss.
     A voice in the crowd
     Cried, "That's not allowed."
Which then ruined her deep state of bliss.

A brazen old voyeur named **Fritz**
Loved to leer at girls with big tits.
     His wolf whistle was loud,
     If one appeared in a crowd,
And he'd shout out, "You thrill me to bits."

A pain-seeking masochist **Dave**
To his lover became a sex slave.
     When she brandished her whip,
     With a quivering lip
He cried, "Mistress, you know what I crave!"

"Yes, I'd like to have sex," said young **Jill**,
"Though I've neither condom nor pill.
     So it'll be up my bum
     If you're wanting to come.
But I'm sure that will give you a thrill."

A gorgeous Adonis called **Piers**
Would leave lovely ladies in tears.
     They seek to pursue him,
     They eagerly woo him
Then find out he's one of the queers.

Said his lover, "That is enough!"
As they lay entwined in the buff.
     "It's great that you ride me
     But don't come inside me.
I've no wish to end up the duff."

Both my brother and I fancied **Sarah**.
We thought no girl could be fairer.
     She frowned and she sighed,
     "I can't really decide."
So we wondered if we could share her.

What can you make of old **Vaughan**?
He's up all night until dawn.
     What gets into his head
     That he won't go to bed?
I think that he's downloading porn.

An eager domestic called **Stan**
Said, "I'm not sure when it began
     But what gets me on heat
     Is a female's bare feet
So I'll be any lady's footman."

A young gigolo who's called **Abel**
Has become something of a fable.
     He's had sex in a bar,
     In many a car
And on his dining room table.

I encountered naive young **Lorna**
And felt that I needed to warn her.
    "Watch out for that boy,
    It may well be his ploy
To get you alone in a corner."

An attractive judge in her gown
Faced a small time crim from her town.
    She said, "Let me say,
    Today is the day
When you learn what it's like to go down."

At a retirement home lives old **Reese**
Who's taken a fifteen year lease.
    Three widows a day
    Call in and then stay
And don't give him a moment of peace.

"I have a new interest," said **Jonah**.
    "I've decided to be a sperm donor.
    Websites that are sleazy
    Will make it so easy
To get a bloody big boner."

Said a precocious student called **Millie**,
"I really think it's so silly.
    I'm dating this boy,
    He's excessively coy
And doesn't let me ...."

The final line should be a climax, a punch line, but I seem to be stumped. I'm afraid Erato, the muse of poetry, seems to have deserted me. I can't think of the last three words. Is it 'boil his billy', 'chop his chilli,' or 'gild his lily'? They all seem too tame. Perhaps readers can think of something more appropriate and punchy.

The following was changed due to censorship:
Said a young Ausssie farmer named **Chuck**,
"I'm terribly down on my luck.
    But I don't care a bit
    That my life's full of misfortune
'Cos my sheila's* a fabulous conversationalist".

* 'sheila' - Australian slang for a woman, just as 'bloke' is for a man. Can be used in a derogatory manner.

ALCOHOL

A social young lady named **Jenny**
Was forever spending a penny.
      The reason is clear,
      She loves to drink beer,
And it's not just a few, no, it's many.

In the pub sat beer-loving **Jim**
With a look that was angry and grim.
      When I asked, "Why the face?"
      He said, "It's a disgrace,
My mug's never filled to the brim."

When I took a beer to old **Fred**
He started to go off his head
      And said with a wail,
      "You know I hate ale.
Go get me a whisky instead."

At the church talented pianist **Hugh**
A sizeable audience drew.
      But he came on so pissed
      He messed up his Franz Liszt
And puked over all the front pew.

What can we make of poor **Daisy**?
Her ramblings are vague and so hazy.
      She appears to be pissed
      Or perhaps round the twist.
Either she's sloshed or she's crazy.

When he rolled home drunk late at night
His partner confronted poor **Dwight**.
      She then showed him the door
      Saying, "That's the last straw.
Clear out, you sad load of shite!"

Said that passionate beer maker **Lou**
Who was rapt with his latest home brew,
      "You can ignore all the rest.
      This is really the best
And I'm sure you will all think so too."

Various Vices: Crime, Gluttony, Greed, Sloth, Love of money, etc.

"Je suis sexy," said dashing **Pierre.**
"See how chic are the clothes that I wear."
      He then pranced down the street
      But tripped over his feet
And suffered a bruised derriere.

That quarrelsome lady **Elaine**
Does nothing but cause us all pain.
      She'll stand on her rights
      And is quick to pick fights.
I'm sure she will drive us insane,

1. A talented forger named **Verna**
Copied the paintings of Turner.
      When she put them on line
      In six months she sold nine
And thought, "It's a hell of an earner."

2. Said the judge as he sentenced poor **Verna,**
"In this case we shall have to be sterner.
      Since she shows no remorse
      There is only one course -
Three years in gaol, that'll learn her!"

Said mercenary minded young **Max**
When approached by two newspaper hacks,
    "If you pay me two grand
    I'll tell you first hand
And acquaint you with all of the facts."

A lazy young fellow named **Bob**
Could never stay in one job.
    He hasn't a goal,
    And he's now on the dole.
That's Bob with no job, what a slob.

Now **Ken** was an excellent cooper
Whose barrels were really quite super.
    But each day, I'm afraid,
    He kept losing trade
'Cos he ceaselessly swore like a trooper.

A conceited fellow named **Bart**
Thought he was ever so smart.
    But we hold the view
    That he hasn't a clue
And he's just a silly old fart.

The **old judge** was bombastic and tedious,
Though his words were weighty and serious:
    "You break every rule,
    Your conduct is cruel
And your actions are highly egregious."

I don't know what to do with my son.
Law breaking to him is such fun.
　　Don't mix with that lad
　　Or you'll turn out bad.
He's a guy everybody should shun.

I have an unruly daughter
Who's never done as she ought-er,
　　She wastes all her time,
　　She dabbles in crime -
A wonder the cops haven't caught her.

A fun-loving playboy called **Sonny**
Thought his life would be all milk and honey.
　　'Til one day he awoke,
　　Found out he was broke
And sadly wailed, "Where is my money?"

Said that brilliant detective **DL**,
"I've a method that works ultra well -
　　Dot the Ps and cross the Qs,
　　Put together all the clues -
And I'll soon have the crim in a cell."

*In homage to Reginald Hill, author of Dalziel (DL) and Pascoe, made
into a popular TV police drama.*

FOOD

A gardening guru named **Jean**
Had fingers incredibly green.
     She grew every berry,
     Pear, pineapple, cherry
And also the odd runner bean.

A gluttonous fellow called **Gus**
Grew to be an XXL plus.
     Now because of his size,
     Whenever he tries
He can't get through the door of the bus.

"I'd eat nothing," said waif-like **Suzanne**,
"Except cold baked beans from the can.
     But when I got mange
     I vowed I would change
And now heat them in a sauce-pan."

An over-weight glutton called **Reg**
To his doctor made this firm pledge:
     "For the sake of my heart
     A new diet I'll start
Which includes two fruit and five veg."

A barbeque wizard called **Stan**
To heat up his grill he began.
     Prime steak for his love -
     Then heavens above!
She let on she was a vegan.

Said an overweight lady **Louise**,
"I'm particularly partial to cheese.
      I eats pounds a day
      But I'm sorry to say
That it makes me continually sneeze."

At my dinner poor sensitive **Di**
Let out this heart-rending cry,
      "He was a good friend
      And he's met a sad end."
All this when I served her lambs-fry.

Said a fastidious eater called **Vicky**,
When offered some tea with a bicky,
      Nice, Digestive, Marie,
      They do nothing for me.
So excuse me for being so picky."

A connoisseur of cheeses was **Claud**.
In his home he amassed a great hoard.
      Their delights he'd expound
      When friends came around,
Which left them a teeny cheese bored.

Said a health-conscious lady called **Greta**,
"I always end meals with some feta.
      I just love its taste
      And there's n'er any waste.
And I'm sure I have never felt better."

Exclaimed a hard drinking old glutton,
"I'll soon feel as bright as a button
    With wines to uncork,
    Beef, chicken and pork
And a tasty roast leg of mutton."

A sedentary lady called **Nellie**
Spent all her days watching telly.
    She kept eating chips
    Which expanded her hips
And gave her a whopping great belly.

"I tried that new restaurant," said **Rick**,
"Though I wish I'd not made such a pick.
    The food was so pricey,
    Excessively spicy
And when I got home I was sick."

A greedy old woman from **Cheddar***
Would **gorge** on all that was fed 'er.
    It made her so fat,
    That when found on a mat,
I'm afraid she couldn't be deader.

Cheddar Gorge, a limestone gorge in the Mendip Hills, near the village of Cheddar, Somerset. The gorge is the site of caves where Britain's oldest human skeleton, Cheddar Man, estimated to be 9000 years old, was found in 1903

MUSIC AND OTHER ARTS

That brilliant soprano **Marie**
Climaxed with a piercing high C,
      Which ignited her gown,
      Brought the house down
And shattered the trunk of a tree.

A saxophonist who is called **Dot**
Played jazz exciting and hot.
      When we all wanted more
      And shouted, "Encore!"
We were told that that was our lot.

Said the teacher to talentless **Max,**
"You'll just have to face up to facts.
      For music, it's clear,
      You just haven't an ear
And you never will master that sax."

An impoverished artist called **Gina**
Was forced to take a job as a cleaner.
      She said, "This damned chore
      Is one hell of a bore."
And since then no one has seen her.

At the fair a budding actor called **Ruth**
Walked into the palmist's dark booth,
      Who said, "You'll go far,
      You'll become a great star."
And **Ruth** wondered, "Could this be the truth?"

A budding young writer called **Belle**
Said, "Have I a story to tell?
     It's all about ghosts
     And I'm certain," she boasts,
"It'll scare everybody to hell."

(autobiographical?)
A wanna-be poet named **Dave**
Thought his rhymes were one hell of a rave.
     But we think his verse
     Couldn't be worse
And he is an out and out knave.

CHESS & OTHER SPORTS

Said that lowly ranked player **John Cook**,
"I'm particularly fond of the rook.
      But it's always the same,
      At the start of each game,
I move them up and they quickly get took."

Be afeared when you play chess with **Jack.**
He's possessed of a formidable knack.
      His play is so strong
      That when you go wrong
He'll quickly have you on the rack.

"Before I start," said nervous young **Kelly,**
"I've rumblings inside my belly.
      If my nerves I could tame,
      I'd win every game,
Even though my legs shake like jelly".

That short-tempered chess player **Wally**
Lost a game through his own careless folly.
      He picked up his king,
      Gave it a fling
And it landed next day down in **Collie.***

*Collie, an inland town in Western Australia, mainly known as a coal-producing centre. It is over 200 kms from the capital Perth where Wally plays.

Here's an enthusiast for three different games and the problem that ensues:

Versatile **Vernon's** in a mess
With a problem he needs to address.
      He wakes up every day,
      Asking, "What do I play?
Is it bridge, is it tennis, or chess?"

A passionate chess player was **Claud**.
Over puzzles daily he poured.
      Giving long explanations
      To all variations,
He left us a little chess bored.

Mitch boasted he'd be Man of the Match
But on most players he wasn't a patch.
      When dropped from the side
      Sadly he cried,
"I don't seem to come up to scratch."

A must-win young sportsman called **Pete**
Was asked why he never got beat.
      "I crush all the rest
      Because I'm the best.
And when I am not - then I cheat."

Said an obstinate batsman called **Paul**,
"I play a dead bat to each ball.
      My motto in cricket
      Is 'don't lose your wicket'.
That's why they all call me 'Stonewall'".

A cross-country runner called **Keith**
Was leading the pack on the heath.
       But then, sad to tell,
       He tripped and he fell
And broke nearly all his front teeth.

That fiery footballer **Fred**
In matches would often see red.
       If losing the game,
       His team mates he'd blame,
Which made them all wish he was dead.

An ultra-fit sportsman called **Mike**
For two hours had raced on his bike.
       He'll then swim fifteen k,
       But won't call it a day
'Till he's finished a three day long hike.

"It's summer," said plumpish young **Kim,**
"And I aimed to go for a swim.
       But maybe you've heard
       This plan I've deferred
Until I can get myself slim."

At the river sporty young **Owen**
Thought he'd like to go rowin'
       But his boat hit a bank
       And it rapidly sank
For he didn't see where he was goin'.

A carefree young fellow called **Dale**
Decides he will go go for a sail.
       But he's now up shit creek
       When his boat springs a leak
And he finds he's not loaded a pail.

Said the coach to golf loving **Lee**,
"Do you know why your drive hit that tree?
       I can see at a glance
       I can sort out your stance.
It'll suit you down to a T."

Said a health conscious fellow called **Jim**
Whose weight was a worry to him,
       "With a daily work-out
       I'll stop being stout
And I'll soon have a body that's trim."

In 1588 a Spanish fleet of 130 ships was sent to invade England. Upon receiving news of the approach of the Spanish Armada, Sir Francis Drake and Lord Charles Howard attacked with 40 superior warships and prevented the invasion. Legend has it that Drake was in the middle of a game of bowls and wanted to finish before taking to sea.

Reading a young student's History exam I found the following malapropism, a supposed quote of Drake when informed of the approach of the Armada: "The Spaniards can wait but my bowels can't."

> While playing bowls upon Plymouth Hoe
> **Sir Francis Drake** was called to go
> > And fight the Dons upon the sea.
> > But he replied, "I'm not yet free.
> Our foes can wait but my bowels, no!"

This reminds me of an anecdote about another English naval hero, **Horatio Nelson***:*

"Admiral, there are three French ships on the port bow preparing to attack."

"Hardy, go and bring me my Admiral's red jacket."

"But won't this make you more conspicuous to the enemy?"

"Perhaps, but if I am wounded the French won't know."

(a little later)

"Admiral there are six French ships on the starboard bow preparing to join the attack."

"Hardy, go and bring me my brown breeches."

ODDITIES

A simple-minded young lady named **Pam**
Thought the ticket she bought for the tram
> Would bear her away
> To the US of A
Where she would meet Uncle Sam.

That angry protester young **Anna**
Marched in a belligerent manner.
> When a policeman came near,
> With no hint of fear,
She whacked him on the head with her banner.

An unfortunate fellow named **Ray**
Would snore once his head hit the hay.
      So to be out of our reach
      He slept on the beach.
Then the tide came and washed him away.

That sweet little lovely **Lorraine**
Made a kite from both paper and cane.
      When she took it to fly
      She arose in the sky
And there for three days did remain.

An attractive young hippy called **Carol**
Would dress in outlandish apparel.
      She once went to a ball
      Dressed in nothing at all
Except for an empty beer barrel.

A slap-happy fellow named **Ross**
Was told by his dentist to floss:
      "Just do as I say
      And comply every day.
Remember, with teeth I'm the boss."

Said his wife to ugly old **Dave**,
"You really must have a good shave.
      With your 'tache and your beard
      Everyone is afeared.
They think you've climbed out of your grave."

Poor **Sidney** fell off his ladder
And it seems he couldn't be sadder.
    He's lying in bed
    With a badly bruised head
And he's lost control of his bladder.

Beth thought there was nothing to harm her,
No dangers ahead to alarm her.
    So she went on the walk
    And got into a talk
With a guy who knew how to charm her.

A problem beset troubled **Lisa,**
For hot summer nights didn't please her.
    She'd toss and she'd turn,
    And feel that she'd burn.
The solution? She'd sleep in the freezer.

There was a young mystic called **Lance**
Who was asked if he wanted to dance.
    He replied with a smile,
    "Can you wait for a while?
I must first put myself in a trance."

At the beach a shy maiden **Gertrude**
Said, "I don't really think I'm a prude.
    But when friends suggest,
    Be it real or in jest,
I refuse to sunbathe in the nude."

"I have a great owner called **Greta**,"
Said a very contented red setter.
    "I sleep on her bed,
    Have walks, am well-fed.
In fact, life couldn't be better."

Last year's Queen of the Pageant **Lolita**
Once more thinks there's no one to beat her,
    Despite also-rans
    Hatching devious plans
Which they'll use to try to unseat her.

Said a contented ascetic called **Mark**,
"Each day I get up with the lark.
    I eat the right foods,
    I don't get in bad moods
And I'm always in bed before dark."

"I'm angry," said **Caroline Cox.**
"Since taking a course of botox
    I suffered such pain
    And what did I gain?
A face that looks like a fox."

"I'm unhappy," said old beanpole **Ted**.
"I can't sleep in this B & B bed.
    You've noticed, no doubt,
    My legs sticking out
Which stop me from bumping my head.

Said a feather-brained lady called **Pru**,
"I rarely know what to do.
    I feel such a dope,
    I know I can't cope
And so often I land in the stew."

Said the doctor who examined poor **Shane**,
Who'd been plagued by an endless migraine,
    "The diagnosis, I fear,
    Is irrefutably clear.
It shows that you don't have a brain."

Said a portly health convert called **Kim,**
"I've started to go to the gym.
      With a work-out each day
      I'm well on the way
To becoming athletic and trim."

A formidable figure is **Mary**
Who lugs the milk churns at the dairy.
      She's tall, strapping and broad,
      She's fiercely square-jawed
And her arms are muscled and hairy.

A besotted young lady called **June**
Exclaimed, "My wedding's real soon."
      But the cad never tarried
      So she didn't get married
And missed out on a planned honeymoon.

At a test a new **bell-ringer** hopes
That he'll reveal how well he copes.
      He huffs and he puffs
      But some changes* he muffs
And is told, "Go home, learn the ropes."

* *changes - ringing the bells in different sequences to produce tunes.*

A rebellious teenager called **Chrissy**
With her folks would get into a tizzy.
>>Said her mum with a frown,
>>"It won't get me down.
She's typically just a young missy."

Poor pain-intolerant young **Bert**
Tripped over and fell in the dirt.
>>He let out a cry,
>>"I'm sure I shall die,
My whole body's so horribly hurt."

A timid youngster who is called **Mark**
Pitched a tent in a National Park.
>>But during the night
>>He ran home in fright
For he found he was scared of the dark.

A new computer user is **Bec.**
She admits she's not fond of new tech.
>>"I hate it," she cries.
>>"It gives me strained eyes,
A sore shoulder and such a stiff neck."

Said an excited astronaut **June,**
"I'll take my first flight very soon.
>>Reach for the stars,
>>Touch down on Mars
And then I'll be over the moon

WESTERN AUSTRALIAN PLACE NAMES

Said an on-line young dater from **Broome**,*
"I'm going to be a bridegroom."
        But the girl got a shock.
        Now she's back in Bangkok
After seeing the state of his room.

A cheeky young schoolgirl called **Hettie**
Played ball upon **Busselton Jetty***.
        A voice from the crowd
        Shouted, "That's not allowed."
She retorted, "Stop being so petty."

Quarrelsome old **Kerry** decided to sue
A crowd of neighbours all from **Cue**.*
        "They treat me real bad,
        It makes me so mad.
And that's why I do what I do."

__Broome,__ a pearling and tourist town, situated in the tropical north of Western Australia.
__Busselton,__ a popular holiday destination in the south west. Its Jetty is the longest timber-piled jetty in the southern hemisphere at 1841 metres long.
__Cue,__ a small town in the Mid West of Western Australia, 620km north east of Perth, with a population of less than 200.

AND FROM THE PERTH SUBURBS

A naive young girl from **Dianella**
Was dating a two-timing fellow.
      That he was untrue
      Of this we all knew
But wondered if we should tell her.

Said a doctor who works in **Balcatta**,
"You want to know what is the matter?
      The answer is plain,
      You're not really sane.
In fact you're as mad as a hatter."

Said the doctor who works in **Balcatta**
To a patient who'd chatter and chatter,
      "Let's have much less talking
      And do much more walking.
That'll stop you from getting much fatter."

An unfit young man from **Carlisle**
Ran a race that measured a mile.
      He couldn't go fast
      And was easily last.
But he still could manage a smile.

An unruly lad from **Kenwick**
At a store window hurled a brick.
        He was nabbed by a cop
        As he ran from the shop
And finished that day in the nick.

A cougar called **Eve** from **Bayswater**
Had designs on the young hotel porter.
        With her come-hither smiles
        And experienced wiles,
He was led like a lamb to the slaughter.

An inquisitive miss from **Bullcreek**
Was impelled to take a wee peek.
        When asked, "What's it to you?"
        She said, "It's something I do
For I'm known as the town's sticky-beak."

A young postie from **Canning Vale**
Was facing a formidable gale.
        But he did his utmost
        To deliver the post
Despite being lashed by the hail.

Said an occasional walker called **Zac**
Who planned to take on the **Bibbulman Track**,
        "Though overweight and unfit,
        I'm possessed with true grit
And intend to give it a crack."

*The Bibbulman Track in Western Australia stretches almost 1000km
between Kalamunda, a suburb of Perth, and Albany, on the south coast.*

A young lady jumped into **Lake Monger**
Where she met a friendly old conger.
      Said her friend, "That's unreal!
      How does the eel feel?"
She replied, "Like a man, only longer." *

** A variation on 'An Aussie girl diving off Tonga' (The Great Australian
Book of Limericks). Lake Monger is a large urban wetland in Perth,
Western Australia, nestled between the suburbs of Leederville, Wembley
and Glenadalough.*

POLITICS

Nine Australian Prime Ministers

Gough Whitlam, Labor PM 1972-75. Whitlam was dismissed by the the Queen's representative, Governor-General Sir John Kerr, after the Upper House, the Senate, refused to pass the budget bills.

> The Governor-General to the Prime Minister
> Said in a tone that sounded quite sinister,
>> "You've no dollars nor cents,
>> So, **Gough**, get you hence.
> You've no longer a realm to administer."

Bob Hawke, Labor PM 1983-91. A charasmatic politician, Hawke broke down in tears at the Memorial Service at Parliament House for the victims of the Tianamen Square Massacre in Beijing. He once held the record for being the fastest to down a yard glass of beer at Oxford University.

> A popular PM is **Bob**,
> Though he's been seen to let out a sob.
>> He loves to drink beer,
>> So let's give him a cheer,
> For he's the best man for the job.

Paul Keating, Labor PM 1991-96. Treasurer and Deputy PM in Hawke's government. The Kirribilli Agreement (Kirribilli House was the PM's official Sydney residence) was to pave the way for Hawke to retire after the 1990 election allowing Keating to become PM. However Hawke reneged on the agreement but a second challenge for leadership by Keating was successful in 1991.

A wannabe-PM called **Paul**
Was annoyed Hawke wouldn't play ball.
Bob said, "You must learn
To wait for your turn."
But this didn't go down well at all.

John Howard, Liberal PM 1996-2007. Howard was the second longest serving Australian PM. In 1995 he pledged to 'never, ever' introduce a GST. However the GST, a 10% tax on most goods and services, was introduced by his Government in 2000.

Little **John** said that the GST
As an impost would 'never, ever be'.
But when re-elected
This tax he selected,
Burdening you and burdening me.

Kevin Rudd, Labor PM 2007-2010 & 2013. *'Kevin 07' romped home in the 2007 election but, with growing dissatisfaction with his performance within the Labor party, he was replaced by his deputy Julia Gillard. He returned as PM briefly but Labor lost the next election and Rudd retired.*

> For the Labor boss **Kevin Rudd**
> The votes flowed in like a flood.
> > But his party had doubts
> > And so threw him out,
> Deciding that he was a dud.

Julia Gillard, Labour PM 2010-2013. *The only woman to become Australian PM. Her plans to introduce a mining tax in 2012 caused an outcry from the mining industry. Combined with other controversial policies, this resulted in loss of popularity and the Labor party replaced her with her predecessor Kevin Rudd.*

> "My mining tax," said ex-PM **Julie,**
> "Made all the rich miners unruly.
> > Twiggy and Gina*
> > Could not have been meaner
> And that was the end of Yours Truly."

*Andrew 'Twiggy' Forrest and Gina Rinehart, two of the leading wealthy miners in Western Australia, who led protests against the tax.

Tony Abbott, Liberal PM 2013-2015. Often portrayed in the media in his 'budgie-smugglers' (Australian slang for men's anatomy-hugging-type swimwear), Tony Abbott was accused in Parliament by Julia Gillard of being a misogynist (woman-hater).

That colourful ex-PM **Tony**
In his bathers looked strong, fit and bony.
    Called a misogynist,
    He screwed up his fist,
"Such a claim is utterly phoney!"

or

Budgie smugglers are his chosen swimsuit.
In these **Tony** thinks he's looks cute.
    Called a misogynist,
    He raised a clenched fist
And cried, "Such a slur I refute."

***Malcolm Turnbull, Liberal PM 2015-2018.** A millionaire merchant banker and former barrister, Turnbull was a late entant into politics. He headed the Republican movement and supported climate change measures, putting him offside with his more conservative colleagues. Consistently poor ratings led to challenges, bringing about his resignation.*

> 'Mr Harbourside Mansion' is glum.
> "Who's that?" you may ask. It's **Malcolm**.
>> A sustained rating drop
>> Saw him given the chop,
> So he now sits at home on his bum.

***Scott Morrison, Liberal PM 2018-.** New leader Morrison steered the Liberals to a surprise victory in the 2019 election but planning for surpluses had to give way to reacting to both the disastrous bush fires in the eastern states and COVID 19 outbreaks.*

> New leader **Scomo** was elated
> When his government got reinstated.
>> But bush fire conditions
>> And COVID restrictions
> Saw all future planning frustrated.

*To minimise the risk of the spread of the corona virus into Western Australia, the state premier, **Mark McGowan,** set up a 'hard border' which, with some exceptions, banned international and inter-state visitors to WA. Despite having mining interests in WA, the Queensland billionaire businessman, **Clive Palmer,** was refused permission to enter the state. He then unsuccessfully challenged the legality of the state's hard border policy in court. He also intended to claim over $30 billion dollars for a decision by a former WA Government and personal insults from the present WA Premier.*

That litigious fat businessman **Clive**
Said, "For however long I'm alive,
    I'll sue any man
    Who hinders my plan,
Even if my vast wealth takes a dive."

Our popular premier **Mark**
Said to Clive, "Stay out of our park.*
    Don't mess with our state,
    Or you'll find out, mate,
That our bite is worse than our bark."

* *Much of the mining in WA is carried out in National Parks or on Aboriginal land.*

ON HOT WEEKENDS

Western Australia enjoys long periods of summer weather with temperatures sometimes above 40°C. Naturally for thousands the beach is a popular place to enjoy the sun.

On hot weekends in this sunkissed land
We flock in droves to our fine white sand.
And it's into the water for a dip,
But be careful to avoid the rip (a).

And that's not all we have to fear.
White pointers (b) might be lurking near.
The jellyfish and sand flies sting
And sea gulls steal the food we bring.

Now if you want to take a nap,
Dont forget the 'Slip, Slop, Slap', (c)
Or you'll be burnt from head to feet
And feel exhausted from the heat.

a) RIP - a rip current is dangerous to swimmers as it is difficult to identify, can occur in good weather and can drag a swimmer out to sea.
b) WHITE POINTER - the great white shark can grow to 6 metres long. They have been responsible for attacks on swimmers and divers around the coasts of Australia, sometimes resulting in death. From 2000 to June 2020 there were 16 fatal attacks in Western Australia.
c) SLIP, SLOP, SLAP - a slogan to encourage Australians to take precautions against sunburn and the possibility of skin cancer. Suncream, hats and also the covering of other parts of the body are encouraged.

A cafe then with ocean view?
You'll wait for hours in the queue
And you'll so wish you had thought twice,
When you sit down and see the price.

So when it's hot I do not roam,
But stay in air-conditioned room
With beer and tele - that's the ticket -
Watching the flannelled fools play cricket.

SHALL WE, SHAN'T WE?

Summertime and close to the sea,
What better place for you and me?
At sunset what about a drink?
Though perhaps you need a second think.
There may be violent gangs around
Who'll roughly throw you to the ground.
"Give me your phone and phone code too
Or we will all lay into you."
Kicks to the ribs, stomps to the head,
The sand around you turning red.
No police around to intervene.
An ambulance bears you from the scene.
A crime statistic is now your fate
With name, address, the site and date.

(inspired by reports of anti-social behaviour and crime at beachside suburbs in Perth, Western Australia)

The Australians are renowned for their love of sport and have a fiercely competitive nature which can generate intense feelings.

AN AUSSIE MATE

Jack's furrowed brow creased in a frown.
"The bloody telly's broken down.
The footy game we cannot view.
Now what the hell is there to do?"

I looked around through the air of gloom
And saw in the corner of his room
An old chess set, perhaps his son's.
"I've seen a way we'll still have fun,
That's if you can play the game,
Though I'm none too sure – it needs a brain."

"Ha, bloody ha, I'm no one's fool.
At chess I was the best in school.
So, if it is a game you're seekin',
Let's go ahead – you'll cop a beatin'".

For Jack and me, our friendship long
Was spiced by competition strong,
For we'd played each other countless times
At tennis, golf and other games.
But never did we ever guess
We'd sit down to a game of chess.

I held two pawns, he picked the black,
Giving me first chance to attack.
My skilful play, such were my hopes,
Would soon have Jack upon the ropes
And, faced with my superior game,
This braggart would be put to shame.

With copious supply of beer to drink
To oil our brains, to help us think,
Each searching for a winning plan
We strove to find the better man.

Taunts and jeers, whose motivation
Sought to ruin concentration,
On us two foes had no effect
As we attempted to select
The moves that would surely bring about
The rival army's utter rout.

The game progressed, move after move,
And desperately I tried to prove
That I was by far the better man
And Jack was just an also ran.

But then I sensed my plans were failing.
Sadly my bright hopes were fading
And, with my forces dissipated,
The likelihood of being mated.
Now don't you laugh, it is no joke
To lose to that obnoxious bloke.

I searched and searched but I could not
Find a move to stop the rot,
'Til finally my concentration
Lit a spark of inspiration.
There was one chance, a trap I'd set.
He'd fall right in, on that I'd bet.

My strongest piece moved to attack,
Bringing a swift reply from Jack.
His gloating smirk was plainly seen
As he reached out and snatched my queen.

"The game is up, accept your fate.
You're a beaten man so give up mate."
No, Jack," I smiled, "our little war
Has culminated in a draw
And we must BOTH accept our fate -
Your final move produced stalemate."

Jack got up and without a word
Swept all the pieces from the board
And, as they clattered to the floor,
He pointed me towards the door.
I left and thought, "It's such a shame,
Our friendship ruined - stupid game!"

The days went by, I felt so blue.
It seemed that nothing I could do
Could break the deadlock or could mend
The mateship with my erstwhile friend.

But now weeks later, I can report,
We're back together playing sport
With confidence that there won't be
Another rift 'twixt Jack and me.
But there's one game, I must confess,
Remains off limit, and that's chess.

REGRET

Chess, like any other sport, has the joy and elation in winning an important game balanced by the despair at a loss, particularly from a position of strength. This poem, describing the agony of losing, was inspired by my final game in England before leaving for Australia in 1972. I had won the County of Cornwall Championship twice before and was hoping to win a third time in my final tournament in the UK.

The final round,
The chance of realisation of a long cherished ambition.
A draw could be
The stepping stone to self fulfilment.
For my opponent only a win would suffice
To usurp my soon to be enthronement.

We play,
My steady hand hiding the gnawing tension within.
The hours pass.
Now no thought of draw
As my queen's side attack brings
My opponent to near resignation.

But lurking near is another foe
Whose face is now tormenting,
Threatening to wrench from my grasp
The merited reward.
That foe, the clock, ticking, ticking increasing loud,
Reminding me of the need for haste,
Filling my mind with doubt,
With panic,
Destroying the ability to concentrate.

Each move I now make with increased fevered force
Betrays my hatred of this soulless adversary.
With seconds left I make the final move
To meet the time control.

My body relaxes,
But only for an instant
For my opponent, with an expression
Of relief, amazement and glee,
Sweeps his queen across the board –
An unstoppable mate!
My reluctant insincere hand extends
To shake that of the usurper,
The regicide.

I rise.
I leave that arena with heavy disbelieving steps.
For my opponent the satisfaction, the elation, the glory.
For me only the might have been –
Nay, should have been –
A regret to remain within my soul,
Sadly and quietly, dwelling on unactual realities.

The chess clock consists of siamese twin clocks with buttons to stop one clock while starting the other. Their purpose is to avoid a player overly delaying a game. Its first use was in the 1883 London tournament, the Tumbling Clock.

I played for many years with an Analog Clock which showed time used by each player. Each face would have a flag which would be picked up by the minute hand as the hour approached before being released when the hour was reached. The clocks might be set at 4.30 and a player required to make at least, say, 36 moves before the flag fell at 6.00. Failing to do this would result in a loss. Having completed his 36 moves a player might then be required to reach move 60 before the clock shows 7.00.

The analog clock was replaced in the 1970s by the Digital Clock which works back from, say, 90 min to zero. A further development was the Fischer Clock, which is in general use today, which can give players a small increment of time (from 2 to 30 sec) after each move. This enables a player short of time to avoid losing on time if he moves quickly, eg with 12 sec left and he moves in 8 seconds, he will then have 4 + 10 sec (if 10 sec is the increment) left for his next move. The Fischer clock is particularly appropriate for fast chess, especially Blitz with a time limit of all moves in 5 min or less but with 2 or 3 sec increment.

Chess Clocks, Digital, Tumbling, Analog

Besides wanting to win my final game and tournament in the UK, I also had the chance of finishing my cricket there on a winning note. Coming in at number 10 to join the opening bat, I hit a 4 to bring the scores level. "Here", I thought, "was my chance to score the winning run in my final innings". Sadly I was yorked next ball and, with the number 11 fending off a bouncer to slips his first ball, the game finished a tie.

CHESS NONSENSE

HOW INTELLIGENT ARE DOGS?

A regular patron at a public house would bring his dog with him and the two of them would have a game of chess.

Another patron remarked to the owner, "What an amazingly intelligent dog you have."

"Intelligent? Intelligent you say? No, he's downright stupid. We've been playing for six months, I give him a queen start each game and he still hasn't won once."

SECOND BOOK?

I've been asked if I'm planning to follow up with second book. I'm toying with the idea of a selection of my howlers over more than 50 years of play but haven't done anything except think of a title, 'Ellis in Blunderland'.

ELLIS IN BLUNDERLAND

Copy of oil painting of author by Jill Williams,
entrant for Black Swan Art Prize,
a premier Western Australian art competition.

IS CHESS RACIST?

There have been claims that chess is racist because White always moves first. Some years ago I wrote: 'The Swiss Parliament will debate a motion next week for a ban on the teaching of chess in all the country's schools. Supporters of the motion maintain that chess, with its warlike associations, is not in keeping with the nation's peace-loving image, that chess may cause some youngsters to have an unhealthy fixation on the game to the detriment of their studies, that playing chess encourages unhealthy rivalries, causes psychological harm to the regular losers and damages racial harmony by pitting white against black.'
This was written April 1, 2011!

CHESS AND MEMORY

In Sao Paulo in 1925 famous chess Grandmaster Richard Reti broke the then world blindfold chess simultaneous record by playing 29 opponents at one time without sight of the board. When he left the playing hall he left his familiar green briefcase behind. When it was returned to him he exclaimed, "Oh, thank you. I have such a bad memory."

His notorious absentmindedness led fellow Grandmaster Savielly Tartakower to remark, "Where Reti's briefcase is, there Reti isn't."

COVID FROM THE SUBLIME
TO THE RIDICULOUS

HERO

Like thousands of his countrymen,
He fought bravely during his nation's struggle
Against an evil foe,
Enduring the privations and dangers of the battlefield.
But you will not find his name among the few
We call our war heroes.

But he is a hero,
Remembered not for leading an attack,
Nor rallying his outnumbered men
To hold off the fearsome enemy hordes,
Nor rescuing wounded colleagues under fire.

He was not a hero on the sporting field,
Standing out among his team,
Or, as an individual, performing with such brilliance,
Winning cups and medals for a success-hungry nation.

He was not strong in body,
Nor muscled and fleet of foot.
He did not climb mountains,
He did not swim seas
Or sail the world alone.
He was not flung beyond the far horizons of space.
He did not endure persecution, imprisonment or torture.
But he is a hero.

Aged and infirm,
He summoned all the strength of his ancient feeble body
To walk, not the length of a country,
But just that of his small garden.
For three dogged weeks he shuffled up and down,
Up and down that short restricted area
With walking frame his sole companion.
Hour after hour, day after day, he plodded on
Striving to raise £1000 for his country's health.

But news of his endeavours could not be contained,
His quest winning the plaudits of an admiring world,
A world bedevilled and frightened by a hideous plague.
Donations pouring in from far and wide,
£33 million to fight this insidious invisible foe,
Donations to honour this old man, this legend, this hero.

"Please always remember," he said,
Tomorrow will be a good day."
Summoned to attend the queen,
A sword gently tapping his shoulder.
"I knight thee, Sir Tom More."

Sir Tom Knighted and promoted to colonel

His hundredth year attained,
Sadly he too was taken by this worldwide scourge.
But he will be remembered,
Sir Tom, hero.
And when that good tomorrow comes
We shall still remember
Sir Tom, hero.

THE OLD MAN AND THE VACCINE

"Our vaccines are successful,"
Proclaims each covid lab.
So I go and see my doctor
To ask about a jab.

He seeks to reassure me
And put me at my ease.
He says he'll answer questions
About this feared disease.

The first question that I ask him,
"Are there side effects
That leave a patient suffering
With severe defects?"

"I'm glad you've asked that question
And got it off your chest.
You really have no worries.
These vaccines are the best."

"Now my wife is nearly eighty
And I am eighty-three.
There's a personal question
Concerning her and me.

"Now I hope this second question
Will not you perplex.
Once I've had the vaccine
Can she and I have sex?"

"No worries," says the doctor,
"I can put your mind at rest.
Your sex life will be normal.
Just put it to the test."

So happy with this answer
To my second question
I then roll up my sleeve
Without hesitation.

This news is so exciting,
It fills me with delight.
I'll tell my anxious partner
And we'll enjoy tonight.

Though it still is hard to credit
For, by my estimation,
It's now been nearly fifteen years
Since my last erection.

The Anti-Vaxxer

Said an angry protester **Max,**
"Don't you dare bombard me with facts.
Your restrictions are harsh
So I'll go on the march
And I'll thumb my nose at the vax."

BELIEVE IT OR NOT

It was the year of 45, the famous 8th of May.
Peace in Europe had been signed, at last our VE Day.
For me and for my comrade no longer must we fight.
We'd join in the celebrations and party through the night.

Thousands had come to London Town, joy was in the air.
No more a time of misery, of terror or of care.
A new era had begun, a time of hope and peace,
And all the noise of battle at last would quickly cease.

The masses flocked to the palace gate to see our much loved king
Together with his family and our anthems we did sing.
And then the crowds in joyous mood were dancing in the street.
The pair of us were hoping two pretty girls we'd meet.

The King, Queen and Princesses
Elizabeth and
Margaret together with Prime Minister Winston
Churchill appearing before the crowds.

Suddenly we saw approaching, without a man in tow,
Two lovely fresh-faced maidens and our hopes began to grow.
One was in her uniform – she told us how she'd served.
I listened most intently but felt somewhat unnerved.

Her manner so exquisite, her diction so refined,
Clearly a class above me but she didn't seem to mind.
We danced and kissed that evening, I hoped 'twould never end,
Longing that she would soon become more than a casual friend.

I began to feel such yearning, my comrade felt the same.
We imagined the girls upon our beds – there was no sense of shame.
But far too soon these maidens said, "It's time for us to go."
We pleaded with them too remain but they firmly answered no.

The years have passed, my gait is slow and my hair has now turned gray,
But pictures of that maiden come to my mind each day.
And I wonder if she remembers the soldier from that night
And that brief but happy dalliance before she fled from sight.

And who is this lovely maiden I knew so fleetingly?
I've ne'er again met up with her but I've seen her frequently.
She's loved and well respected, she appears on the tv.
She's now in her eighties, to her we bend the knee.

She is our dearest Head of State residing in palace grand,
And thousands long to meet her and kiss her on the hand.
But of her loyal subjects few can voice the claim
That they have flirted with the Queen, Elizabeth her name.

You've listened to my verses since my tale began,
A young and gorgeous princess, a common serviceman.
Now if you believe this story, with envy you'll turn green,
For you never had the pleasure of snogging our dear Queen.

(inspired by a BBC documentary on VE Day.
The princesses Elizabeth and Margaret were allowed by their parents, King
George and Queen Elizabeth, to leave the palace and mingle with the crowd.)

JOHNNY BE QUICK

I wrote the following poem and adapted it to the Chuck Berry song 'Johnny B Goode'. Together with a soprano, Alessia Pintabona, a chorus of my daughter's son and daughter, we recorded the song for my son John on his 41st birthday in 2019, the year he became Asian Trail Running (Ultra-Marathon) champion with four course victories during the season. Races were run throughout Asia, some up to 160km long, with temperatures reaching 40° on occasions.

From an early age John seemed destined to be a long distance runner. Before his third birthday, on a walk of about two miles around the Garrison on St Marys in the Isles of Scilly, he declined to get in a pusher. Even before that, soon after he had learnt to walk, he accompanied his mother and me to the tavern in Yanchep, a northern suburb of Perth, where I was playing in a chess tournament. The event was held in a downstairs room and it was the first time John had seen stairs. These proved a fascination as he walked up and down the steps, up and down, up and down, up and down, holding his mother's hand.

Aged about 11 he climbed to the top of Mount Snowdon, the highest mountain in England and Wales. At Little Athletics his speciality was the longest race, the 3km walk, gaining medals at West Australian state championships. At school it was cross-country and after that marathons including the New York Marathon. Yet he wanted more of a challenge and progressed to ultramarathons with distances sometimes more than three times that of the marathon, usually with mountain climbs.

Way up on Hong Kong island, close to China's shore,
There lives an Aussie runner whom we hold in awe.
No distance can be over-long for this young man to run,
A hundred k's or more and he thinks it is such fun.
He'll travel the world over so he can compete.
He's determined, fit, athletic and so very hard to beat.
In USA and Africa, in Hong Kong and Japan,
In Europe and Australia too are places that he ran.

Chorus after each verse:
    Go! Go! Go, Johnny, go! Go, go, Johnny, go, go!
    Go, Johnny! go, go! Go, Johnny, go, go!
(v1, 2) Johnny, be quick! / (v 3) Johnny be **good!**

He'll run both in near freezing cold and in the searing heat.
Whatever he is faced with, that challenge he will meet.
The terrain it may be rocky and the going rough,
But all that hardly matters because he's built so tough.
He's well prepared and ready for each gruelling race.
He'll follow his well thought out plan and set a steady pace.
Then he'll decide to make a surge, when he knows it's time,
And overtake his rivals to reach the finish line.

We may wonder at his lust for speed.
What makes this running such a need?
Why is he so prepared to face
The challenge of each gruelling race?
But now another passion, he's since become a dad.
The birth of little Maxie has made him feel so glad.
And now with dearest mum Elaine he will never rest,
For parenting, like running, demands one's very best.

JOHNNY KEEPS ON RUNNING

Some years earlier I had similarly arranged the song 'Felix Keeps on Walking' (words Hubert W. David, music Ed E Bryant).

Chorus:
Johnny keeps on running, keeps on running still.
With the pack behind him you will always find him.(a)
They want to surpass him but his shoes they cannot fill.
And Johnny keeps on running, keeps on running still.

In blazing sun or pouring rain,
Through every kind of rough terrain,
Speeding past each sign
Until the finish line.
Up hill or mountain, on track or road,
In the heat or freezing cold.
And no matter where he goes
He's always keen and on his toes.

Throughout the world our Johnny ran,
In US, Africa, Japan.
Back in Australia too
With challenges anew.
With stamina and grit so strong
No distance was for him too long.
And where there is a race to win
He just can't wait to begin.
      CHORUS

a) He would not in fact take an early lead but would wait until half way or later to start a surge towards the front.

When democracy was the people's aim
Their demonstrations gained world fame.
While thousands in the streets did sit
Johnny also did his bit -
A run a hundred k m long
Throughout the regions of Hong Kong.
With his friend Andrew by his side
He took this challenge in his stride (b)

(spoken)
Running running for hours and hours,
No time to stop and admire the flowers.
The scenery along the way
Will have to wait another day.

b) In 2014 a worldwide publicised run of over 100 km in the shape of an umbrella, the symbol of the Hong Komg protest movement.

We follow his exploits with awe
As he forges on with muscles sore,
A great example to his peers
That well deserves our heartfelt cheers.
Now take a break to hear our song
Before you once more run along.
And Happy Birthday, dearest son,
Our king of the Ultra-Marathon.

CHORUS
So, Johnny, keep on running, keep on running still.
With the pack behind you we shall always find you.
They want to surpass you but your shoes they cannot fill.
So, Johnny, keep on running, keep on running still.
Keep on running, keep on running, keep on running still.

*(photos by permission of the South China Morning Post,
Hong Kong, and BC Magazine, Hong Kong.)*

A SCILLY CHILDHOOD MEMORY

Isles of Scilly

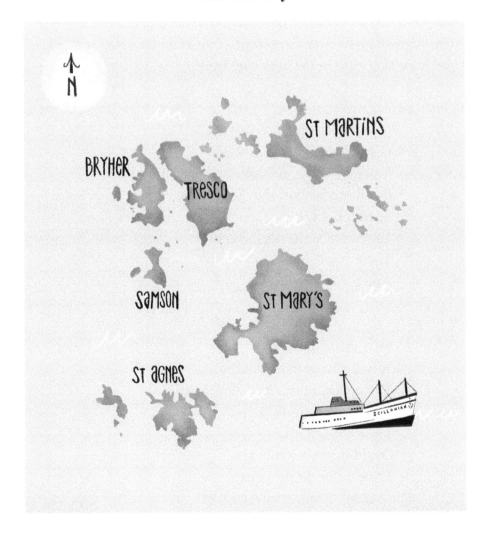

My childhood, before going to the mainland of Cornwall to attend secondary school, was spent on St Marys, the largest of the Isles of Scilly (pronounced silly), 42km (28 miles) from Lands End, Cornwall, an idyllic place to live, especially for children enjoying their summer holidays from school. The year 1947, when I was seven years old, provided a particularly warm and dry summer, giving day by day sunny weather to enjoy. However the words of the poet Henry Wadsworth Longfellow, immortalised in song from the Ink Spots with Ella Fitzgerald, 'Into each life some rain must fall', are pertinent to the following verses.

I were born on the Scilly Isles,
Off Britain's far south-west.
You may think the name sounds funny
But those islands, they're the best.
Spelt S C I L L Y,
To remember here's the key,
There is a C in Scilly
And Scilly's in the sea.

Now the summer of 47
Was such a wondrous time,
The opportunities it gave us boys
To run about and climb
The trees, go fishing
Or riding on our bikes,
To take dips in the ocean
And enjoy long country hikes.

My mother runs a village shop (a)
Selling cigarettes and sweets.
She knows each customer by name
And each she warmly greets.
In summer there is a constant flow
Of customers each day,
For my mother's home-made icecream
Could not be beat they say.
And often when the sun was hot
And I'd been running round the town,
I'd pop in for a vanilla cone
To help to cool me down.

I'd come home tired and dusty
As happy as could be,
And when I saw my granny
I'd ask her, "What's for tea?"
Whatever was put before me
Would quickly disappear
And when dessert was offered
I'd scoff that up, no fear.

(a) The shop, Trenwiths, was owned by my aunt, my mother's sister.
The sisters ran the shop for much of the 1940s and 1950s.

But some days I'd want a change
From hectic times with mates
And I'd wander down to the quayside
Where my grandad's boat awaits.
He was a strong and burly man
But kind and full of smiles.
His boat, the Nor Nor, would ferry goods
To and from the smaller isles.

*The Scillonian, the Penzance to St Marys
ferry, with the Nor Nor alongside about to
be loaded with cargo for the Off Islands.*

Cap'n Bob

On a short trip to St. Martins,
Where my old grandad was born,
He took me with him for a walk
Into the little town.
And there I saw to my surprise,
After we'd walked a while,
All dressed up in their Sunday best,
The folk of that small isle.

We were going to a wedding,
In church we sat in pews
And I noticed boys who looked so smart
In clean shirts and polished shoes.
But me, I had no shirt nor tie,
No shoes upon my feet,
Just a pair of grubby shorts
Which I wore in the summer heat.
I imagined the congregation
On me their eyes did train
And I shrank as small as I could be,
Filled with embarrassed pain.

And after church the wedding feast
More misery did bring.
Delicious food was piled sky high
But I could hardly eat a thing.
The jollity went on and on.
The end, when would it come
When I could get back on the boat
And finally reach home?

And when we did at last return
Unto St. Marys quay,
Standing there before us
My mother I did see.
No pleasant greeting welcomed me
As she grabbed me by the ear.
The angry look upon her face
Made me quake with fear.

"He should have been home hours ago.
I've been searching high and low.
That he was in your keeping,
Of that I didn't know."
The smacks rained down upon my legs
And my tears flowed in a flood.
My grandad tried to intervene
But it didn't do no good.
"The fault it was entirely mine
So vent your rage on me."
But his words on her had no effect
As she ignored his plea.

Then miserable, sore and hungry,
I were ordered to my bed.
The memories of that sad day
Remain inside my head.
But the details of my escapade
In that long distant time
Have given me this opportunity
To share my tale in rhyme.

CAP'N BOB

"Robert Ellis, or Cap'n Bob, as he was generally referred to, was born on the island of St Martins.....He served as captain of the Nor Nor and later the Kittern and was well known for going out in the most appalling weather, both between the isles and, when needed, the mainland. He would regularly take the smaller launches back (and forth) to Penzance when (the regular ferry boat) the Scillonian was laid up for her annual refit (a one way trip of 60 km or 37.4 miles).

'The twelve-ton motor launch Kittern of the Isles of Scilly Steamship Co., the charge of Mr Robert Ellis, Capt. Bob, arrived at Penzance on Friday 17th November during a gale. On board were 40 boxes of flowers and mail but no passengers.'

Capt. Bob was well known as a skilful and intrepid seaman for whom duty and a sense of obligation to the off-islands (the four inhabited islands smaller than St Marys) and their needs came first.

He retired on 30 December 1950; in all he worked on the islands for over 40 years. He died in 1968 at the age of 87."

(from the publication 100 years of the
Isles of Scilly Steamship Co.)

He was also for a number of years a member of the lifeboat crew responsible for many rescues in atrocious weather.

CORNWALL AND THE SCILLIES

Said a shivering chappie called **Billy**,
"I must find a place that's less chilly.
The name might seem funny,
It'll cost heaps of money
But I think I'll be moving to **Scilly.**"

A pirate who hails from **Penzance**
Was once plagued by St Vitus Dance.*
He hipped and he hopped
But never once stopped
All the way from Cornwall to France."

St Vitus Dance is a disorder characterised by rapid uncoordinated jerky movements.

GUY FAWKES

I've recently seen this quotation in my local paper The West Australian: 'The last person to enter Parliament with honest intentions was Guy Fawkes'. Guy Fawkes (1570-1606), who had fought for Spain in the Netherlands, joined an unsuccessful plot to assassinate King James I. Around midnight on November 4, 1605, Guy Fawkes was discovered in the cellar of Parliament with 36 barrels of gunpowder. He and others involved in the plot were tried and executed for treason. The failure of the plot is celebrated in England each year on November 5 and known as Guy Fawkes Night or Bonfire Night when an effigy of Guy Fawkes is burnt on a bonfire. In my childhood children would be able to set off their own fireworks although in our present day more safety-conscious society this practice has given way to large organised extravagant displays. However the celebration is in danger of disappearing and being replaced by Halloween.

'Remember, remember the fifth of November,
Gunpowder, treason and plot.
I see no reason why Gunpowder Treason
Should ever be forgot.'

These words of 1645 were attributed to John Milton, the author of Pilgrim's Progress. He served as a public servant in the Commonwealth, the republic set up after the English Civil War following the defeat of the Royalists and the trial and execution of King Charles I.

This poem was first written while in primary school but has been altered and put to music together with a chorus. The original began - 'One day when watching the birds in the trees, Guy Fawkes thought up a spiffing wheeze.' ('spiffing wheeze', probably words used in the Billy Bunter stories by Frank Richards). It also contained the lines, 'Next day Guy Fawkes is still at large. He's got his headquarters in a little garage.' Clearly I then knew very little of the actual historical facts and wasn't worried by anachronisms.

The story of Guy Fawkes to you all I will sing.
It happened in England when James One was the king.
To blow up Parliament was Guy Fawkes' intent
And so to some bad men secret letters he sent.

Chorus after each verse:
Oh what a plan, oh what a plot, oh what a blaze there will be!
Oh what a plan, oh what a plot! It will go down in history.

Now Guy Fawkes had studied which way to go
When he had blown up Parliament and so
Having put gunpowder down in the cellars,
Said to his henchmen, "Be quiet, you fellows!"

A chappie comes down to see what's about
And when he sees Guy Fawkes he gives out a loud shout,
"To arms! To arms! There are some bad men down here.
They're going to blow us up, I do fear!"

The Government is in one heck of a state.
Guy Fawkes, though frightened, shouts to one of his mates,
"Come on, come quickly! Let us get out this way.
We'll leave our exploding until some other day."

A man hunt has started throughout our fair land
But that traitor Guy Fawkes can still not be found.
No, crafty old Guy Fawkes is still on the run
And in a new hide-out he is planning more fun.

"Next time we must succeed in our task,
But first let us dry this wet gunpowder cask".
They put that wet barrels by the fire to dry,
(LOUD EXPLOSION)
And this is the reason we still have our Guy.

Printed in Australia
AUHW020547010622
364413AU00001B/4